W9-AVK-042

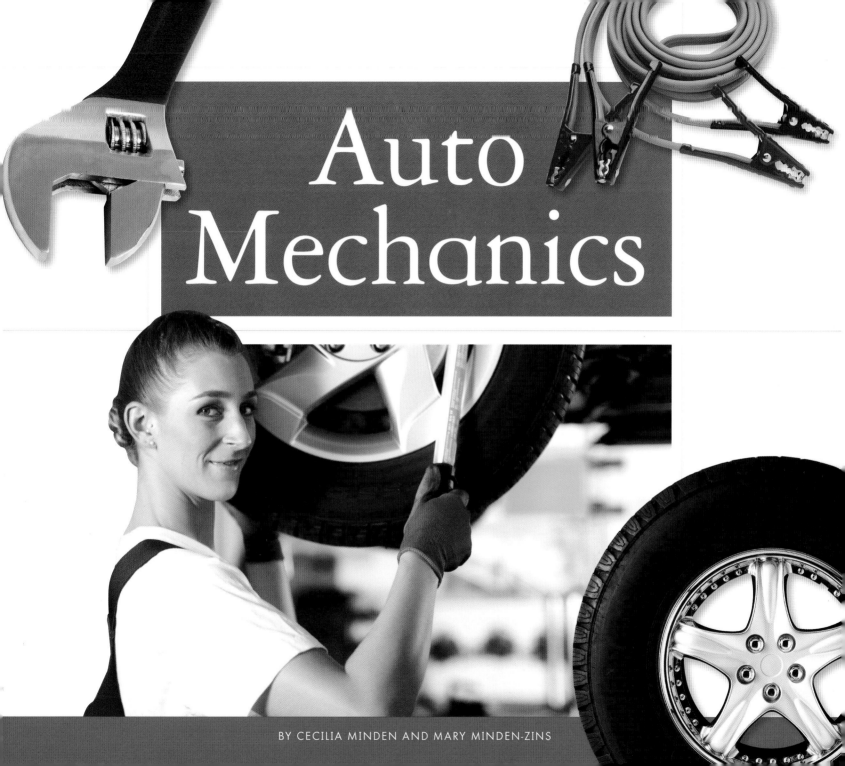

Auto
Mechanics

BY CECILIA MINDEN AND MARY MINDEN-ZINS

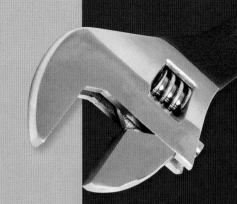

The Child's World

Published by The Child's World®
1980 Lookout Drive • Mankato, MN 56003-1705
800-599-READ • www.childsworld.com

Acknowledgments
The Child's World®: Mary Berendes, Publishing Director
The Design Lab: Design
Jody Jensen Shaffer: Editing
Pamela J. Mitsakos: Photo Research

Photos
Arne9001/Dreamstime.com: cover, 1; carlofranco /
iStock.com: 20-21; Fred Sweet/Shutterstock.com:
5; herreid14/iStock.com: 22; IS_ImageSource/
iStock.com: 10-11; kali9/iStock.com: 6-7; Karol
Sobolewski/123RF.com: 17; monkeybusinessimages /
iStock.com: 12; PhotoDisc: design elements; RichLegg/
iStock.com: 4; Shannon Fagan/123RF.com: 8; Steve
Mann/Shutterstock.com: 18; Ugo Ambroggio/123RF.
com: 13

ISBN 9781626870093
LCCN 2013947287

Printed in the United States of America
Mankato, MN
November, 2014
PA02251

ABOUT THE AUTHORS

Dr. Cecilia Minden is a university professor and reading specialist with classroom and administrative experience in grades K–12. She earned her PhD in reading education from the University of Virginia.

Mary Minden-Zins is an experienced classroom teacher. She taught first grade for ten years before taking time out to raise her children and grandchildren. Mary now teaches kindergarten and lives in Oklahoma.

CONTENTS

Hello, My Name Is Javier.

Hello. My name is Javier. Many people live and work in my neighborhood. Each of them helps the neighborhood in different ways.

I thought of all the things I like to do. I like using my hands. I like to figure out how things work. I like looking at different cars. How could I help my neighborhood when I grow up?

I Could Be an Auto Mechanic!

Auto mechanics are very good at figuring out how things work. They know how to use their hands to fix things.

Best of all, auto mechanics get to be around all kinds of cars!

When Did This Job Start?
The American Motor Company opened a repair garage in New York in 1899. Repair garages soon opened in other large cities. Repair garages were all over the United States by the mid-1950s.

Kids who enjoy fixing things might make good auto mechanics.

Learn About This Neighborhood Helper!

The best way to learn is to ask questions. Words such as *who*, *what*, *where*, *when*, and *why* will help me learn about being an auto mechanic.

Where Can I Learn More?
Automotive Service Association
PO Box 929
Bedford, TX 76095

National Institute for Automotive
Service Excellence (ASE)
101 Blue Seal Drive SE
Leesburg, VA 20175

Asking an auto mechanic questions will help you learn more about the job.

Who Can Become an Auto Mechanic?

Boys and girls who want to know about cars and how they work may want to become auto mechanics. People who want to be auto mechanics also need to know how the different parts in a machine all work together.

How Can I Explore This Job?

Does a parent or other adult you know work on cars? Ask if you can watch or maybe help. Work on fixing your own bicycle. You'll become familiar with some of the tools mechanics use.

Auto mechanics are very important to the neighborhood. They make sure people's cars are working the right way. It would be hard for people to get to work and school if they didn't have working cars.

Auto mechanics make sure that people have working cars.

Meet an Auto Mechanic!

This is John Ahooei. John is an auto mechanic in Oklahoma City. When John is not at his shop, he likes to spend time with his family. He also loves to play soccer.

How Many Auto Mechanics Are There?
About 818,000 people work as auto mechanics.

John Ahooei works as an auto mechanic in Oklahoma.

Where Can I Learn to Be an Auto Mechanic?

John went to the University of Oklahoma, but people don't have to go to college to become auto mechanics. They can work with people who are already auto mechanics and learn how to fix different cars. They can also go to **vocational schools** that offer classes for auto mechanics.

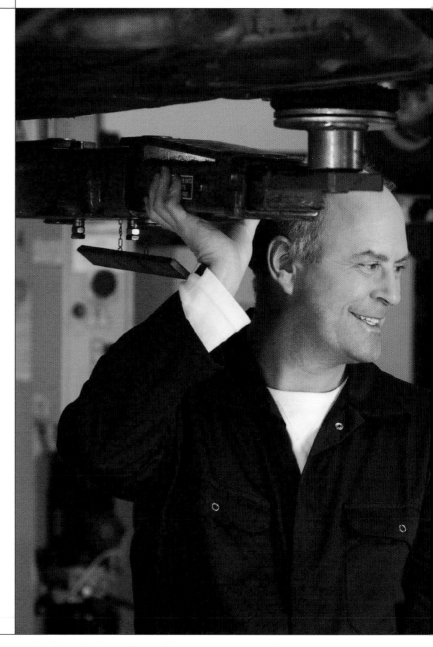

Students get hands-on training at vocational schools. They work with tools they will one day use as auto mechanics.

John still takes classes to learn new and better ways of working on cars. He wants to be sure his customers get the best service.

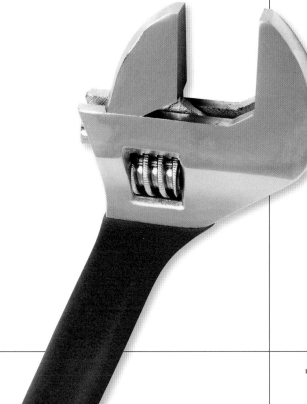

How Much School Will I Need?

Most auto mechanics have high school diplomas. Many mechanics have taken more classes at vocational schools and passed tests. These mechanics are then given certification. Someone who gets certification proves they have the abilities to work in a certain profession.

Students learn a lot at vocational schools.

What Does an Auto Mechanic Need to Do the Job?

A car has many parts that must all work together to make it run safely. An auto mechanic has to know the name of each part and which tools can be used to repair it.

What Are Some Instruments I Will Use?
- Computerized testing machines
- Hand tools
- Power tools

There are different tools for different parts of a car.

One set of tools John uses is called a **socket and ratchet set**. John's tools must be very strong so they do not break when he is working on heavy machinery.

A very important car part is the car battery. Do you have a toy car that uses a battery? A car battery is much larger because it needs to give a real car more power. John has to know how to take out an old battery and put in a new one.

Where Does an Auto Mechanic Work?

John has owned John's Auto Shoppe for fifteen years. It is a small business with four auto mechanics. John teaches his workers to treat each car as if it were their own.

Four mechanics work at John's Auto Shoppe in Oklahoma City.

John's day begins when a customer brings in a car for repair. John has to figure out what's wrong with the car. He spends time talking to the car's owner. John also asks if the car is making any odd sounds.

John tries to figure out what is wrong with the car. He may call an auto parts store so he can get a new part to replace the old one.

John then goes to work on the car. After the car is fixed, he takes it for a **test drive.** John returns the car to the customer if the test drive goes well.

How Much Money Will I Make?
Most auto mechanics make between $22,000 and $41,000 a year.

Welders in body shops fix dents from accidents.

Who Works with Auto Mechanics?

John fixes many cars, but sometimes other people help his customers, too. Workers at a body shop often repair dents and other damages caused by accidents. John also knows people who do the detailing on cars. They help cars stay in good shape by carefully cleaning them inside and out.

What other Jobs Might I Like?
- Aircraft mechanic
- Automobile collision repairer
- Bus and truck mechanic
- Motorcycle mechanic

When Does an Auto Mechanic Get to Work on a Race Car?

Some auto mechanics are specially trained to take care of race cars. It is important for auto mechanics who work on these cars to know a lot about them. Race cars often need special parts. Auto mechanics have to know how to fix all of these parts. Wouldn't it be fun to take a race car for a test drive?

How Might My Job Change?
Mechanics may eventually work with specific systems or parts of a car. Other mechanics may open their own businesses.

Some auto mechanics take care of race cars.

I Want to Be an Auto Mechanic!

I think being an auto mechanic would be a great way to be a neighborhood helper. Someday I may be the person fixing your car!

Is This Job Growing?
The need for auto mechanics will be about the same as for other jobs.

Why Don't You Try Being an Auto Mechanic?

Do you think you would like to be an auto mechanic? You can get practice by learning how to take care of your bike.

Maybe YOU will be an auto mechanic one day!

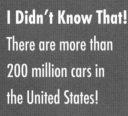

Ask an adult to help you make sure your bike is safe to ride:

- Check the bike seat, handlebars, and wheels. They should fit snugly.
- Check the chain. It should be oiled and move smoothly.
- Check the brakes. They should work well and not stick.
- Check the tires. They should have enough air.

GLOSSARY

socket and ratchet set (SOK-it AND RA-chit SET) a tool set used to tighten and loosen different car parts

test drive (TEST DRYV) when a mechanic drives a car to make sure everything works

vocational schools (voh-KAY-shun-ul SKOOLZ) special schools where people learn skills needed for different trades

LEARN MORE ABOUT AUTO MECHANICS

BOOKS

Flanagan, Alice K. *Mr. Yee Fixes Cars.* Danbury, Conn.: Children's Press, 1998.

Florian, Douglas. *An Auto Mechanic.* New York: Greenwillow Books, 1991.

Korman, Justine, and Steven James Petruccio. *At the Auto Repair Center.* New York: Scholastic, 1999.

Weintraub, Aileen. *Auto Mechanic.* Danbury, Conn.: Children's Press, 2003.

WEB SITES

Visit our home page for lots of links about auto mechanics:

www.childsworld.com/links

Note to Parents, Teachers, and Librarians: We routinely check our Web links to make sure they're safe, active sites—so encourage your readers to check them out!

INDEX